FUNDAMENTAL PHYSICS

Forces
and Motion

GERARD CHESHIRE

A⁺
Smart Apple Media

First published in 2006 by Evans Brothers Ltd.
2A Portman Mansions, Chiltern Street,
London W1U 6NR

This edition published under license from
Evans Brothers Ltd. All rights reserved.
Copyright © 2006 Evans Brothers Ltd.

Series editor: Harriet Brown, Editor: Katie
Harker, Design: Simon Morse, Illustrations:
Q2A Creative

Published in the United States by
Smart Apple Media
2140 Howard Drive West, North Mankato,
Minnesota 56003

U.S. publication copyright © 2007
Smart Apple Media
International copyright reserved in all
countries. No part of this book may be
reproduced in any form without written
permission from the publisher.
Printed in China

Library of Congress Cataloging-in-
Publication Data

Cheshire, Gerard, 1965-
Forces and motion / by Gerard Cheshire.
p. cm. — (Fundamental physics)
Includes index.
ISBN-13: 978-1-58340-995-4
1. Force and energy—Juvenile literature.
2. Motion—Juvenile literature. I. Title.
II. Series.

QC73.4.C515 2006
531'.6—dc22   2005038054

9 8 7 6 5 4 3 2 1

Contents

Introduction

Forces are all around us. When you walk or run, pick up an object, or push a door, you are exerting a force. You can feel the effects of forces, too. Forces change the way things move. Without them, the world would be a very different place.

This book takes you on a journey to discover more about the world of forces and the impact forces have on our everyday lives. Learn about how forces are produced and the effects they have on the objects around us. Discover the amazing force of gravity and how it prevents objects on Earth from traveling into the depths of space. Find out about famous scientists such as Galileo Galilei and Isaac Newton. Learn how they used their skills to explain the effects of forces and how, over time, this knowledge has led to the development of useful machinery.

This book also contains feature boxes that will help you unravel more about the mysteries of forces and motion. Test yourself on what you have learned so far, investigate some of the concepts discussed, find out more key facts, and discover some of the scientific findings of the past and how these might be utilized in the future.

Forces are an essential part of our lives. Now you can better understand why it would be impossible to live without them.

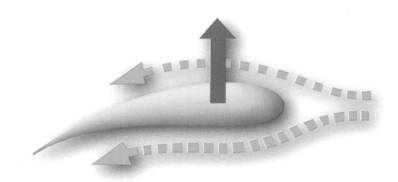

Did you know?

▶ Look for these boxes—they contain surprising and fascinating facts about forces and motion.

Test yourself

▶ Use these boxes to see how much you've learned. Try to answer the questions without looking at the book, but take a look if you are really stuck.

Investigate

▶ These boxes contain experiments you can carry out at home. The equipment you will need is usually cheap and easy to find.

Time travel

These boxes contain scientific discoveries from the past and fascinating developments that pave the way for the advance of science in the future.

Answers

At the end of this book, on page 46, you will find the answers to the questions from the "Test yourself" and "Investigate" boxes.

Glossary

Words highlighted in **bold** are described in detail in the glossary on pages 46 and 47.

1

What is a force?

We may not be able to see them, but forces are a part of everyday life. Whenever you pick up a plate, chew your food, open a jar, or push a cart, you are exerting a force. Forces are exerted on you, too. You'll know about forces if you've ever dropped an object on your foot or have had to struggle against the strength of the wind.

Forces are essentially "pushes" or "pulls," and they change the way things move. You can't see forces, but you can see or feel their effects. The following table shows the effects forces can have on everyday objects.

Forces can cause an object to:	For example:
Speed up	Kicking a soccer ball
Slow down	Using the brakes on a bicycle
Change direction	Hitting a ball with a bat
Turn	Using a can opener
Change shape	Chewing taffy or gum

We give different names to forces depending on the type of effect they have on an object. Several forces can also act upon an object at the same time.

Forces usually act in pairs—if object A exerts a force against object B, object B will exert a force in return. Imagine you are lifting yourself up onto a wall or getting out at the side of a swimming pool. As you push down on the top of the wall with your hands, you exert a force downward onto the wall, but at the same time, the wall resists the force of your hands, which has the effect of lifting you upward. We say that both objects are exerting a force in this case.

Forces occur in pairs, and they are said to be "balanced" or "unbalanced," depending on the effect a force has. A simple example to compare the balance of forces can be seen in a tug-of-war competition. When both teams pull with the same force, there is no movement because the forces are balanced. However, if one team increases its pull, the forces become unbalanced, and the rope moves. An arm wrestling competition is another example (except this time, the forces are moving toward each other). There may be a time when both competitors push very hard, but their arms stay in the same place. Only when one player exerts a greater force does any movement occur.

Balanced forces do not cause a change in **motion**. They are equal in size and opposite in direction. Unbalanced forces, on the other hand, explain the movement we see in the world around us. We use unbalanced forces every day in our lives. Without them, we (and the objects around us) would stay in one position all the time.

▼ These dogs are enjoying a tug-of-war competition. When the force of their pull (shown in red) is balanced, there is little movement. However, if one of the dogs pulls with a greater force, it will move backward, pulling the toy and the other dog with it. Both dogs also exert a downward force on the ground (shown in blue).

◄ When cargo ships are used to move goods around the world, they are carefully loaded to ensure that the goods are not heavier than the upward force of the water. This ensures that the ship will stay afloat.

Although movement is part of our everyday lives, balanced forces are all around us, too. A table stays in one place because the force of **gravity** (see page 14) pulls it down. The table is also pushed up by the ground or the floor that it stands on—the forces are balanced, and the table sits motionless.

If a book sits on the table, it is also pulled down by gravity, but the upward force of the table balances this force so that the book stays motionless. If the the book falls over the edge of the table, the pull of gravity causes the forces to become unbalanced. In the same way, a ship that is overloaded with cargo may sink if it becomes heavier than the upward force of the water, called **buoyancy**.

A balanced force doesn't have to be stationary, however. If an object is already moving, it will continue going at a steady speed if the forces are balanced. However, if unbalanced forces are applied to an object, they may cause it to speed up or slow down. The rate of **acceleration** depends on the size of the force and the **mass** of the object (see page 10).

▲ Unbalanced forces are experienced when you walk on sand. It is difficult to move forward because your feet sink.

TIME TRAVEL: DISCOVERIES OF THE PAST

The Greek philosopher Aristotle was the first person to write down ideas about forces and motion. Aristotle believed that all substances were made from four elements—earth, air, water, and fire. In his view, "natural motion," such as falling, occurred because of an attraction between elements (a stone falls to the ground to be with the "earth," and smoke rises to be with the "air"). Aristotle also thought that animals and humans demonstrated "voluntary motion" because they could choose to move. In addition, "forced motion" occurred because one object forced another object to move.

Aristotle's beliefs were undisputed for more than 2,000 years. Later, however, in the 1500s, scientists such as Galileo began to disprove these ideas. One objection to Aristotle's theory involves an example of a bow and arrow. Aristotle's theory of forced motion stated that objects moved only when a force was acted upon them. So how does an arrow fly through the air when the bow is no longer exerting a force?

▲ Aristotle

In the late 1500s, English scientist Isaac Newton built on Galileo's ideas and declared that motion occurs because of an interaction between two objects. Newton called the cause of this change in motion a "force." Newton's views opposed Aristotle's beliefs that some objects just moved without a cause—in his view, declaring that a stone simply chooses to fall to the ground fails to account for the force of gravity. During his studies, Newton made three "laws of motion" that soon became established and accepted by the scientific community. At the time, many people regarded Newton as the "Father of Physics."

MEASURING FORCE

Forces are measured in poundals or Newtons (N)—named after Isaac Newton. In technical terms, one poundal is the force required to make an object with a mass of one pound (0.45 kg) accelerate with a speed of one foot (0.3 m) per second, every second. A Newton is the force required to make an object with a mass of one kilogram (2.2 lb.) accelerate with a speed of one meter (3.3 ft.) per second, every second. However, on Earth, objects have to compete with the forces of gravity and **friction** when they move. For this reason, scientists also describe one Newton as the downward force provided by a **weight** of 0.1 kilograms (0.2 lb.)—about the weight of an apple.

To explain these problems, Galileo had introduced the concept of "**inertia**." Galileo claimed that an object continues to move unless an external force acts upon it. So, an arrow continues to fly through the air until the force of air **resistance** (see page 23) or the force of gravity (see page 14) slows it down and brings it to the ground.

2

Motion

Forces change the way things move. A force may cause an object to start moving, to speed up, to change direction, or to stop moving altogether. Increasing our knowledge of forces helps us to understand why things move in a particular way.

The effect of forces has encouraged car manufacturers to look carefully at the design of their products. Cars look very different today than they did in the early 1900s. Modern cars are designed partly to look fashionable. However, manufacturers also know more about the way in which a car's design can make it move faster and minimize the amount of fuel that is needed.

◀ ▲ Cars began to be mass-produced in the early 1900s. Over the next 100 years, car design changed as models became lighter and more streamlined to overcome the force of air resistance.

CHANGING MOTION

Speed is a term used to describe how fast something is going—or how far it has traveled in a certain time. When an object increases in speed, it is said to be "accelerating." When an object is slowing down, it is said to be "decelerating." The speed of a car is affected by the power of the engine, the weight of the car or its passengers, and whether the vehicle is moving on a flat road or up- or downhill. The amount of resistance the car is facing (see page 23)—whether friction between the tires and the road surface or the resistance of the air pushing against the shape of the car—is also a factor. The larger the surface area facing the wind, the greater the force the car has to overcome.

In order to look at the different ways that forces affect motion, let's consider a real-life situation. Imagine that Sam is holding a tennis ball that he drops out of the window of a tall building, hundreds of feet above the ground.

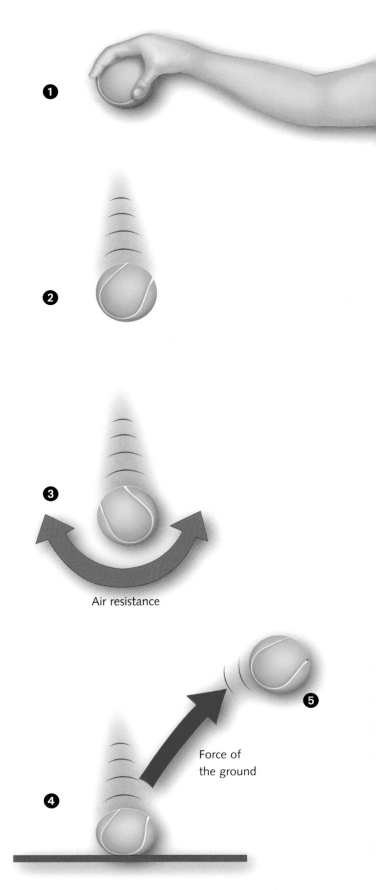

1 When Sam holds the tennis ball in his fingers, ready to be released, it is motionless. Scientists say that the ball is in a state of inertia. Although Earth's gravity is attracting the ball toward the ground, the muscles in Sam's arm and the force of friction between his fingers and the felt of the ball's surface ensure that the tennis ball stays motionless.

2 As soon as Sam releases the ball, the force of gravity pulls it toward the ground, making it fall. As it falls, the ball also speeds up (accelerates) as the force of gravity continues to act upon it.

3 However, while the ball is falling to the ground, **molecules** in the air obstruct its path. This air resistance (or friction) causes the ball to stop accelerating. When the weight of the ball equals the force of the air resistance, the ball begins to fall at a steady speed.

Air resistance

4 As the ball strikes the ground, the force of the impact squashes the ball because the upward force of the ground is greater than the weight of the ball.

5 The force of the ground pushes the ball upward and back into the air, and it begins to bounce a few times before it rolls along the ground and eventually stops moving altogether.

Force of the ground

In the following chapters, you will learn more about the different forces that have caused Sam's tennis ball to move in different ways.

The effects of forces on movement can also be seen in a game of pool. A variety of forces cause the balls to move around the table at different speeds and in different directions. The balls are the same size and weight, and when they collide, there is little friction between them. However, the force of their movement causes the balls to deflect and change direction. If a ball is spinning on impact, it will have a more dramatic effect, moving away at a different angle. This is also true of other ball sports, such as soccer and tennis. Players can make the ball spin so that it travels in a curve or bounces in an unexpected way.

▲ Many sports use the effect of forces. In pool, a cue stick is used to push the balls with a force from the player. If the balls collide, they move away from each other at different angles. The edges of the table also stop the force of a moving ball, causing it to change direction. The table is covered in felt to provide a frictional force as the balls roll along.

TEST YOURSELF

▶ A car travels 155 miles (250 km) at an average speed of 62 miles (100 km) per hour. How long will the journey take?

▶ Take a large marble or steel ball bearing and place it on a small, flat table so that it sits motionless. When the ball is not moving, you are demonstrating that the ball is in a state of inertia. Now, roll the ball along the surface. You will see that the ball moves at a steady speed—this constant speed is also a type of inertia.

▶ If you carefully lift the edge of the table and release the ball down a sloped edge, you will see that it speeds up (accelerates) when it moves because the forces become unbalanced—the force of gravity (see page 14) overcomes the upward force of the table.

▶ Now place the ball at the center of the level table again. Take an identical ball and roll it toward the first. You'll find that when the balls collide, they move apart at different speeds and different angles. The force of the collision and the effects of friction cause the balls to move in different directions.

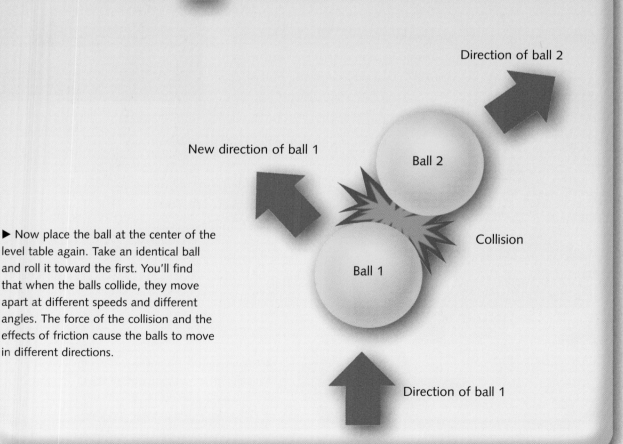

Ball

Level surface

Ball accelerates

Surface tilted

Direction of ball 2

New direction of ball 1

Ball 2

Collision

Ball 1

Direction of ball 1

3

The force of gravity

Gravity is Earth's own pulling force that makes things fall. When you jump up to catch something, you will soon fall back down to the ground again. Even skydivers—who jump from aircraft high above Earth's surface—cannot escape the pull of Earth's gravity.

▶ The moon (top) orbits Earth because it is attracted by a strong gravitational pull.

PHYSICAL ATTRACTION

When we talk about gravity, we usually refer to the strong attraction between objects and Earth. However, gravity is actually a force that causes all objects to attract each other. Isaac Newton (see page 9) was the first person to show that all objects—from apples falling to the ground to Earth **orbiting** the sun—attract each other with a gravitational force .

The strength of gravity depends on the mass of the two objects and how close they are to one another. People and other objects on Earth are attracted to the ground because Earth is so immense (in comparison) and has a strong pull of gravity. Earth itself orbits the sun because it is attracted by the strong pull of gravity from this huge, burning star. However, the moon orbits Earth because, although it is also smaller than the sun, it is closer to Earth and is therefore attracted first and foremost by Earth's pull of gravity.

◀ The moon is 2,160 miles (3,475 km) in diameter—about a quarter of the size of Earth's diameter (7,913 miles or 12,734 km). The average distance of Earth from the moon is 238,600 miles (384,000 km).

ELLIPTICAL ORBITS

The pull of gravity can be very strong, but objects still manage to spin around (or orbit) other planets because their forward motion balances the pull of gravity. Objects in orbit are actually attempting to fall toward the source of gravity, but instead of falling, the speed at which they are traveling causes them to follow a curved motion around the planet. Some planets of our solar system orbit the sun in an elliptical pattern (an oval-shaped pattern rather than a circular pattern). This means that the planets move faster when they get closer to the sun because the strength of gravity increases. The planets then begin to slow down again as they move away from the sun, where the strength of gravity decreases.

▼ The sun is at the center of our solar system and is orbited by nine planets, their moons, and smaller objects such as asteroids and comets. Some of the planets orbit in an elliptical pattern. When they come close to the sun, they speed up under the force of the sun's gravity.

▼ Jupiter is the largest planet in the solar system. It has 16 moons (although more may be discovered). Some of the moons are thought to be asteroids that have been captured by Jupiter's immense pull of gravity.

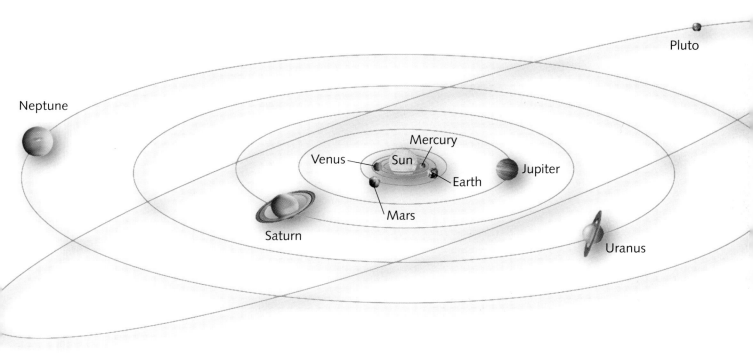

Pluto

Neptune

Mercury

Venus

Sun

Earth

Jupiter

Mars

Saturn

Uranus

▲ ▼ Each day, the oceans rise and fall as the force of the moon's gravity pulls on Earth. There are two high tides and two low tides each day.

THE TURNING TIDES

The sea level changes each day as the **tide** turns. Tides are caused by the moon's pull of gravity on Earth. As the moon passes overhead, the force of gravity literally lifts the ocean water to form a bulge, or "high tide." The same pull has an effect on the land, but because Earth is solid, it doesn't move as dramatically. On the other side of the world, however, the slight movement of Earth (toward the moon) causes the ocean water to rush into the gap, forming another high tide.

As Earth rotates, different points are affected by the moon's gravity. There are two high tides and two low tides each day. The sun's pull of gravity also affects the oceans, but because the sun is farther away, the pull is weaker and becomes noticeable only when it is added to the force of the moon. This happens when Earth, the moon, and the sun are in line with each other (at new and full moons). At these times, the tides are far higher than usual and are called "spring tides." When the sun and the moon are at right angles to each other, the sun's gravity counteracts the force of the moon, and this is when lower "neap" tides occur.

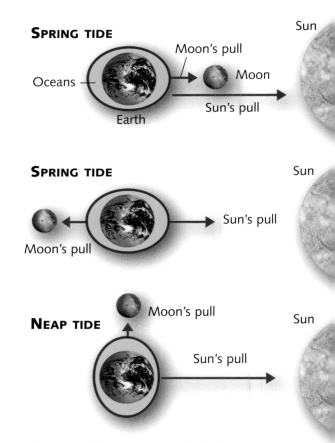

SPRING TIDE — Sun, Moon's pull, Moon, Sun's pull, Oceans, Earth

SPRING TIDE — Sun, Sun's pull, Moon's pull

NEAP TIDE — Moon's pull, Sun, Sun's pull

▲ A spring tide occurs when Earth, the moon, and the sun are in line with each other. This can be when the moon is on the far or near side of Earth. A neap tide occurs when the sun and the moon are at right angles to each other.

MASS VS. WEIGHT

How much do you weigh? Although the terms "mass" and "weight" are often used together, they mean different things in science. Your mass is the amount of "**matter**" (stuff that you are made from), while your weight is the force with which gravity attracts you to Earth. Weight is measured in pounds or kilograms.

An object has the same mass wherever it happens to be. However, its weight can change dramatically. Earth's pull of gravity decreases as you move into space. The force of gravity of other stars, planets, and objects in space also varies with distance. For example, the force of gravity on the moon is weaker than on Earth because the moon is so much smaller. This means that a man weighs six times less on the moon than on Earth. Similarly, on Earth, a large boulder will be heavy and difficult to lift, but on the moon, the boulder will feel much lighter.

DID YOU KNOW?

▶ If you and a friend both weigh about 130 pounds (60 kg) and you stand next to each other, you will be attracted by a force of about seven-millionths of a pound (0.000001 N)!

▼ When astronauts walk on the moon, they are six times lighter than they are on Earth. This is because the force of gravity that attracts the astronauts toward the moon is weaker.

Legend has it that Isaac Newton was sitting under an apple tree when an apple fell on his head, prompting him to think about the effect of gravity. We don't know whether the apple actually fell on Newton's head, but the action of fruit falling from a tree could certainly have encouraged Newton to analyze what he saw.

Newton knew that a force must have caused the apple to accelerate as it fell to the ground. He also knew that even apples from the highest trees fell to the ground in the same way. Newton began to wonder if the force of gravity might reach all the way to the orbit of the moon! He supposed that the force holding any object to Earth was the same force that held the moon, the planets, and the stars in their orbits.

Newton came to the conclusion that any two objects in the universe exert forces of gravity that attract each other. According to Newton's "law of gravitation," the force between any two bodies is related to their mass and the distance between them. Newton's law affects all objects in the universe, from raindrops in the sky to the planets in the solar system. The theory was the first to accurately describe the motion of objects on Earth, as well as the movement of the planets that astronomers had long observed. In fact, Newton's law led to many exciting new discoveries, such as the existence of the planet Neptune. Scientists had noticed variations in the motion of the planet Uranus for many years, and using Newton's law, they predicted that the existence of another planet near Uranus might be causing a gravitational pull, affecting Uranus's orbit. Sure enough, in 1864, Neptune was discovered in an orbit close to Uranus, as predicted.

Newton's theory of gravitation was accepted for many centuries, but over the years, astronomers began to question some of Newton's views. The most notable argument was the fact that the planet Mercury seems to **gyrate** when it orbits the sun—moving to a different position for every complete rotation. In 1916, Albert Einstein helped to explain these differences—but that's another story!

◀ Isaac Newton

Escaping Earth

Humans have always had a desire to explore the world around them. Once they had combed Earth's surface—for lands, continents, and oceans—humans soon wanted to investigate what lay above the skies.

At first, humans used powerful **telescopes** to observe the night skies, but during the 1900s, developments in science and technology meant that the dream of observing space firsthand at last became a reality. **Space probes** began to explore the planets, and eventually people traveled to explore the depths of space itself.

BEYOND OUR PLANET

Since 1972, many men and women from different nations have orbited planet Earth in a **spacecraft**, but no one has yet ventured farther into space. However, many unmanned space probes have explored the solar system, and modern technology is developing so rapidly that it's not unthinkable that astronauts will be able to set foot on Mars before the end of the 2000s.

Unlike space missions to the moon (which take a matter of days), space missions to other planets would take months, if not years, to complete and would require sophisticated life-support systems to make sure that human crews could survive the physical demands and the dangers of constant space travel. A significant number of astronauts have already given their lives in the pursuit of space exploration, but the thrill of discovering more about the depths of space encourages many more to risk their lives.

▲ In the 1960s, the U.S. Mariner spacecraft missions began to explore planets such as Venus and Mars.

Today, many space probes are still orbiting the planets and our sun. In the late 1990s, space probes launched in the 1970s (*Pioneer 10 & 11* and *Voyager 1 & 2*) had traveled between 50 and 100 times farther than the distance from Earth to the sun. These probes continue to send back information via radio telescope, although contact is limited.

Space exploration is developing all the time. In 2004, an unmanned U.S. **satellite** was launched to further investigate the effects of gravity in space. A small privately built spacecraft also rocketed 62 miles (100 km) above Earth's surface. Although the craft didn't achieve a high enough speed to continuously orbit our planet, it was a step toward the possibility of commercial space travel in years to come.

TIME TRAVEL: DISCOVERIES OF THE PAST

1608 – The telescope is invented by Hans Lippershey, a German-born Dutch lens maker. The telescope is introduced to astronomy the following year by Galileo Galilei.

1687 – Having established his laws of motion and gravitation (see page 18), Isaac Newton suggests firing a man-made satellite into orbit with a cannon.

1865 – French science fiction novelist Jules Verne is the first to give the idea of space travel a human aspect in his book *From the Earth to the Moon*. In his stories, Verne invents a "moon gun" that transports his characters to the moon.

1923 – German **rocket** scientist Herman Oberth suggests sending a telescope into space.

1926 – American scientist Robert Hutchings Goddard succeeds in launching the first liquid-fueled rocket (right).

1957 – The Soviet Union's space program comes to life with the successful launches of the *Sputnik* satellites. *Sputnik 1* sends radio signals back to Earth for the first time, and *Sputnik 2* takes the first animal into space—a dog named Laika.

1961 – Russian pilot Yuri Gagarin achieves a whole orbit of Earth in *Vostok 1*, making him the first true astronaut. Less than a month later, Alan Shephard becomes the first American to orbit part of Earth in the *Freedom 7* space capsule.

1962 – John Glenn becomes the first U.S. astronaut when he orbits Earth in *Friendship 7*. The U.S. also lands the first space probe, *Mariner 2*, on Venus.

1962 – The U.S. National Academy of Sciences approves the building of a large space telescope. The Hubble telescope would take 20 years to build but

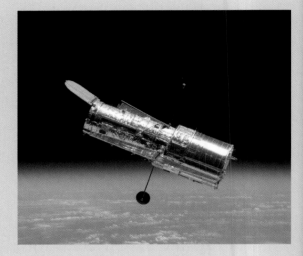

▲ Work on the Hubble space telescope began in the 1960s, although Hubble wasn't launched until 1990.

now orbits Earth, taking powerful images of the universe.

1963 – Russian astronaut Valentina Tereshkova is the first woman in space on board *Vostok 6*.

1968 – Frank Borman, James Lovell, and William Anders become the first astronauts to escape Earth's gravity and reach the moon during the U.S. space mission *Apollo 8*.

1969 – Neil Armstrong and Edwin Aldrin become the first men to walk on the moon.

1981 – The first **space shuttle**, *Columbia*, is successfully launched in the U.S. Space shuttles are designed to carry people and equipment to and from space. However, since accidents in 1986 (*Challenger*) and 2003 (*Columbia*), there are concerns about the safety of these craft. New plans for a series of robotic space shuttles may now take space exploration to another level.

1998 – The first section of the International Space Station (ISS) is launched. The station orbits approximately 225 miles (360 km) above Earth. Although the ISS is still being built, it has been manned with a small crew since 2000, and space research and exploration is already taking place.

5

Friction

Friction is very important in our lives. Without the force of friction, we wouldn't be able to walk without slipping. In a car, friction helps the tires grip the road surface and prevents them from skidding. Friction also acts on the brakes to slow the car down. But friction doesn't always make our lives easier or safer. Sometimes, friction wastes energy and prevents us from moving as fast as we'd like to.

▲ Spiked sneakers help athletes grip the ground without slipping when they want to run fast.

WHAT IS FRICTION?

Whenever an object moves (or tries to move), friction occurs. Friction can cause an object to slow down or to eventually stop. Friction can also change the direction of a moving object by causing it to slow down on one side only (making the object "spin"). Stationary objects are also prevented from moving at all by the force of friction.

There are many advantages to the force of friction. Friction stops objects from sliding past each other. Soccer shoes and spiked sneakers are designed to prevent feet from slipping when running because they increase the frictional force between the shoe and the ground. (In the opposite way, ice skates and skis are designed with a smooth surface that keeps friction to a minimum.) Friction ensures our safety in other ways, too. New car tires have a lot of "tread"—a rough surface that provides grip between the tire and the road surface. Car tires can become worn when they are used, and in time, they need to be replaced— the smoother surface of a worn tire provides less "grip" and will make the car more difficult to control and stop.

▶ Ice skates have a thin, smooth surface that reduces friction between the ice and the blade.

▲ The friction between the moving parts of a machine can produce heat, sound, and light energy. Frictional sparks can also be produced—similar to the spark you make when you strike a match.

But friction also has its downside. Friction between the moving parts of a machine produces heat and sound energy that is "wasted" energy. This reduces the efficiency of a machine. Friction can also wear down parts of machinery that may later need to be replaced. Think of how much an eraser is worn away when you erase pencil markings; just think what friction can do to the moving parts of a machine! Everyday activities require us to overcome the forces of friction, too. If you've ever tried biking against the wind, you know what this is like. Because extra energy is needed to overcome frictional forces, such as air resistance, the maximum speed we can reach on a bicycle is limited.

INVESTIGATE

▶ Next time you go for a bike ride, think of all the ways in which friction is present.

• Friction enables the tires to grip the road surface—without friction, it would be like riding on ice.

• Friction acts on the brakes where they rub on the rim of the wheel. However, the brakes work well only if there is enough friction between the tires and the road—brakes are of little use in icy conditions.

• Friction between parts of your body and parts of the bike—your hands on the handlebars, your feet on the pedals, or your bottom on the seat—enables you to grip the bike without falling off.

• If you bike against the wind, you will find that air resistance (a type of friction) means that you have to pedal much harder.

• Friction also holds the nuts and bolts of your bike together.

AIR AND WATER RESISTANCE

Moving objects on Earth have to pass through air (or water). Air and water are made up of molecules, and these can obstruct moving objects, making it more difficult for them to travel forward. When you walk or run in water—in a pool or at the beach—it is much more difficult than just walking through air. Air molecules can **compress** together, making room for a moving object to pass through, but water molecules cannot compress, so they provide far greater resistance to moving objects.

If air or water molecules are already moving themselves, the resistance can cause an object to travel backward. This happens when the force of resistance is greater than the force of forward motion of the object— walking against the flow of a river or the force of the wind, for example.

To understand the kind of resistance water provides, imagine someone doing a belly flop into a swimming pool, compared to someone diving smoothly into the water. The first diver has exposed more of his body to the water's surface, whereas the second diver passes through the water more easily. This is because only a small area of his body is affected by water resistance.

▲ This diver moves through the water easily because only a small area of his body makes contact with the water.

▼ The force of the wind and flowing water can be difficult to walk against.

SURFACE FRICTION

Although some objects may appear to be smooth, at a microscopic level, they probably have lots of lumps and bumps. When objects rub together, the ridges on their surface collide and create friction. Friction can cause different effects, depending on the roughness or smoothness of the surfaces, the materials they are made from, the other forces involved, and the directions of those forces. Some materials are used particularly for their frictional properties.

WHY ARE WET ROADS SLIPPERY?

Wet roads are more slippery to walk or drive on than dry roads. On a dry road, friction causes the rubber sole of your shoe (or the rubber tire of a car) to "stick" to the road as it moves along. The rubber pushes down into tiny pits found on the road's surface. However, on a wet road, water gets trapped inside these tiny pits as your shoe (or the tire) presses down on them. The water stops the rubber from expanding into the pits—in effect, the water smooths out the surface of the road, reducing friction.

Sandpaper has a very rough surface that is useful for making materials smooth. When you hammer a nail into a piece of wood, friction prevents the nail from slipping out of the wood. Friction also prevents objects from slipping off surfaces that are not level. Next time you are walking up a steep slope, be thankful for the frictional force between your shoes and the ground!

◀ Friction caused by the rough surface of moving sandpaper is used to smooth materials such as wood.

LUBRICANTS

Lubricants are fluid materials that we use to create a film between two surfaces, preventing them from rubbing together. Lubricants reduce friction, and they also prevent the wear and tear that friction causes. The term "fluid" doesn't necessarily mean a liquid, but a material that is made of molecules that are able to flow over one another. Lubricants include gases, water, ice, gels, oils, greases, pastes, waxes, resins, powders, plastics, and even soft metals. Car mechanics put oil into a car engine to help the car work more efficiently and to keep the metal parts from rubbing together and wearing away. Skiers rub wax onto their skis to help them travel faster over the snow. If a ring is stuck on your finger, rubbing a lubricant, such as soap or oil, around the ring will help you to remove it more easily!

▶ We add lubricants to our car engines to keep them working smoothly and to prevent wear and tear.

TIME TRAVEL: DISCOVERIES OF THE PAST

▶ In 1959, British engineer Christopher Cockerell invented the hovercraft (below right). Also known as an "air-cushioned vehicle," the hovercraft has a "rubber skirt" filled with air, which acts as a lubricant between the craft and the surface on which it is traveling (land or water). When air is pushed into the rubber skirt under **pressure**, it fills so that the vehicle "floats." This means that the hovercraft can move forward, backward, and sideways without being affected by surface friction.

▶ Another vehicle that travels on a layer of pressurized air is the ekranoplan (also known as the "screen-plane" or "ground-effect vehicle"). This vehicle, invented in 1961 by Russian engineer Rostislav Alexeev, looks very similar to an airplane but doesn't really fly. Instead, its forward motion traps and compresses a layer of air between the vehicle and the surface below, so that it lifts up, reducing the force of friction. Although the hovercraft and the ekranoplan still have to deal with air resistance once in motion, their clever designs help to keep surface friction to a minimum.

6

Flight and buoyancy

In order to minimize air and water resistance, objects need to be streamlined. Many animals on Earth clearly demonstrate the benefits of a streamlined design—birds have wings that stretch out and cut through the air as they fly, and fish have sleek bodies and fins that help them steer through the water. Manufacturers often turn to these clever designs of nature when they make vehicles such as cars, boats, and airplanes.

THE AIRFOIL

Scientists say that a streamlined object is "aerodynamic" in air or "hydrodynamic" in water. An **airfoil** is a term used to describe an object, such as a wing or a propeller blade, that controls stability, direction, and movement in a vehicle that travels through air. The wings of birds are known in engineering terms as "airfoils." Engineers use a similar design to make the wings of airplanes and **gliders** and the rotor blades of helicopters.

This cross-section of an airfoil shows how it works in more detail. Notice how the shape is streamlined so that air resistance is minimized, although the structure is still sufficiently strong to work without breaking. Notice also how the

▼ Airplanes are heavier than air, but their design creates a lifting force that overcomes their weight. The engines power the movement of the airplane, but lift occurs when moving through air because the wings are streamlined and have a curved surface.

upper surface is curved so that it has a greater surface area than the lower surface. This is a crucial feature of an airfoil.

As the airfoil moves forward, air molecules are forced to travel both over the top and underneath. The molecules traveling below the airfoil tend to become slightly more compressed than the surrounding air and create an area of high pressure. Meanwhile, the molecules traveling above initially become compressed but are then forced to spread out, creating an area of low pressure. The relative difference in air pressure on each surface of the airfoil causes it to move upward. If the machine (or the animal) is light enough, and excessive air resistance is reduced by its design, flight becomes possible.

CROSS-SECTION OF AN AIRFOIL (WING)

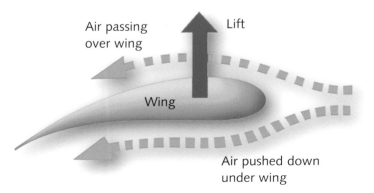

Air passing over wing

Lift

Wing

Air pushed down under wing

PARACHUTES

Parachutes are the opposite of airfoils—instead of minimizing air resistance, they use it to create an upward force against the pull of gravity. Parachutes slow down the fall from a plane. Without a parachute, a person would fall through the air very quickly. However, a parachute provides a greater surface area and has a curved shape to make it difficult for air molecules to pass. This air resistance causes the parachute (and the person) to fall more slowly. A similar principle is used in a **hang glider**, a popular flying device used as a sport. A hang glider looks like a parachute and uses air resistance to bring a glider slowly back down to the ground. However, it also has an airfoil design to enhance lift in rising currents of air.

▼ An open parachute is curved so that it is higher in the middle. This makes it more difficult for air molecules to pass. The air resistance slows down the person's fall.

MOVING IN WATER

Lift cannot be achieved in water in the same way as it can in air. This is because water is a liquid (rather than a gas), so its molecules cannot be compressed or **decompressed** to make areas of high or low pressure. Fish have streamlined bodies that move through the water with the least possible resistance. Some aquatic animals, such as dolphins, have flippers that resemble wings, but they don't share the same airfoil properties. Instead, dolphins rely on their buoyancy (see page 28) to prevent gravity from pulling them downward and their fins to provide forces that help with forward movement and steering.

▲ A dolphin controls its depth by changing the angle of its body and fins as it swims.

THE HYDROFOIL

A **hydrofoil** is a boat with wing-like surfaces, called foils, that sit beneath the hull. As the boat increases its speed, the foils create enough lift for the hull to move out of the water. Because water resistance is kept to a minimum, hydrofoils can move much faster than ordinary powered boats. Most passenger-carrying hydrofoils can travel about 62 miles (100 km) per hour.

▶ Hydrofoils are a useful passenger seacraft because they move so quickly over water.

BUOYANCY

An object will float in water if it has a weight that is equal to the weight of the water that it displaces. This is why a boat can carry cargo across the ocean, but if the cargo were thrown overboard, it would probably sink. The volume of water that is displaced changes according to the amount of surface area the object has in contact with the water. This principle is known as the "law of displacement" and was discovered by the Greek philosopher Archimedes. You can see Archimedes' law in action when you step onto a sailboat. The water level rises on the side of the boat when weight is added. The amount of water displaced by the hull is always equal to the weight of the boat and its contents.

◀ A boat's design enables it to float in water and carry people and goods.

Floating objects exert a downward force on the water, which is counteracted by the upward force of the water. Buoyancy is determined by whether an object is more or less dense than the liquid it is floating in. We say that a boat demonstrates positive buoyancy because it is less dense than water and can float.

When we look at objects that float beneath the surface—such as submarines—we see something different. When a submarine is on the water's surface, it has positive buoyancy. However, a submarine's buoyancy can be altered using tanks filled with air. When the submarine remains at a constant depth underwater, without moving upward or downward, it is said to have neutral buoyancy. When the submarine is made to sink deeper by releasing air, it has negative buoyancy.

▲ A submarine can control its buoyancy using air tanks, allowing it to sink or surface when it needs to.

TIME TRAVEL: DISCOVERIES OF THE PAST

▶ During the 1980s, the sport of ski jumping was revolutionized by an accidental discovery! Ski jumpers used to perform their feat by holding a straight, forward posture over parallel skis. However, in the mid-1980s, Swedish ski jumper Jan Bokloev altered ski jumping forever by introducing his "V" technique. Story has it that during training, Bokloev suffered a slight seizure in mid-flight that forced him into a "V" position. To his surprise he floated farther than ever before! By the 1992 Winter Olympic Games, the "V" technique had become the standard of the sport. Scientists have agreed that aerodynamically, this posture adds a "surface" that the ski jumper can use to float through the air.

Legend has it that Icarus became the first person to fly, by attaching feathered wings to his arms using bees' wax. Icarus is only a character from Greek mythology, but nevertheless, his story is an example of man's early ambition to fly like the birds.

The first man-made device that stayed in the air for long periods of time was the kite. Invented by the Chinese in the 1200s, some kites were even capable of lifting people! Then, Italian engineer Leonardo da Vinci began to draw sketches of a machine that later became the helicopter in the 1900s.

In 1783, two French brothers introduced the idea of the hot-air balloon. Joseph-Michel and Jacques-Etienne Montgolfier built their balloon from paper and linen and used a fire below to fill it with hot air. Their design was clever, but neither brother understood why the hot air made the balloon rise. This knowledge was left to another Frenchman, Jacques Charles, who made a more advanced hydrogen-filled balloon later that year.

British engineer George Cayley discovered the principles of the airfoil (see page 26). Between 1799 and 1804, Cayley built the first fixed-wing aircraft—a model glider—followed a few years later by the first full-sized, piloted glider. By the 1900s, advances in the design of engines meant that it was possible to combine a lightweight power source for a propeller with a glider, turning it into an airplane. Another pair of brothers achieved this feat—American brothers Wilbur and Orville Wright. In 1903, the pair became airborne using a powered aircraft. Then, in 1908, French engineer Louis Berguet built the first helicopter.

▲ The Wright Brothers were self-taught engineers who invented the first powered airplane.

◄ Kite flying is now a popular hobby, but at one time, kites had other uses, too. In the 1890s, kites were used to take instruments into the air that could record weather patterns, such as temperature and humidity. Kites have also been used in times of war to lift people so that they could see the enemy!

THE SHAPE OF THINGS TO COME

The very first airplanes and helicopters were rather crude-looking structures, bearing little resemblance to the machines we know today. But since the early 1900s, streamlining has been perfected in all kinds of transportation. Today's aircraft had their design planned in the early 1900s with the help of French aviator Louis Bleriot and Ukrainian aviator Igor Sikorsky. Their designs used the streamline concept so that air resistance was minimized. A similar change occurred with car design in 1934, with the Chrysler Airflow model, designed by American Carl Breer.

In many cases, streamlining is vital to a vehicle's performance. However, vehicle design also needs to take into consideration the look and practicality of the model—something designers call "styling." This is especially true of road cars, in which streamlining is necessary only if high speeds need to be reached.

▲ Designers of modern aircraft have used their knowledge of streamlining to make planes that can move farther and faster than ever before.

As a result, cars continue to change in shape all the time as people become attracted by a "new look" and feel inclined to replace old models with something more modern. Many cars are now designed with issues of space in mind—enough space to accommodate a family lifestyle or reduced space to make it easier to park in towns and cities.

DID YOU KNOW?

▶ In March 2004, scientists tested an unmanned aircraft that achieved a world record speed for flight. The vehicle traveled through the **atmosphere** at speeds of around 4,970 miles (8,000 km) per hour. Compare this to a family car that reaches speeds of around 75 miles (120 km) per hour.

7

Pressure

Pressure is a force we encounter every day in our lives. The water in your shower and the air in your bicycle tires are subjected to pressure. Like friction, pressure can bring both advantages and disadvantages to our lives. Thanks to our knowledge of pressure, we can chop our food with a sharp knife and use thumbtacks to pin up paperwork on a bulletin board. But pressure can also cause problems. When pressure builds up, it can cause an immense force when it is suddenly released.

WHAT IS PRESSURE?

Pressure is the amount of force that is subjected to a certain area and is measured in pounds per square inch (or pascals). Pressure is greatest when a large force is distributed over a small area—when using a sharp knife, for example. If you push your finger against a wall, you are unlikely to make a lasting impression. However, if you apply the same force to push a thumbtack into the wall, you will make a mark (or a hole). The force is the same in each case, but the thumbtack applies more pressure because the force is concentrated into a smaller area. Likewise, the head of the thumbtack is round and flat to distribute pressure over a large area so that the pin doesn't jab into your finger.

We use our knowledge of varying pressure in other aspects of our lives. For example, modern vehicles now have air bags that inflate on impact. In the event of an accident, the air bag spreads the impact of the force over a larger area so that injuries are minimized or prevented. In a similar way, goods that are transported are often wrapped in air-filled plastic to reduce the impact of any bumps in transit that could damage the goods.

◀ Air bags are now a common safety feature in modern road vehicles. The bags help to minimize injury by spreading the force of an impact.

▲ Magma erupts from a volcano because it tries to escape from the pressure that has built up under Earth's surface. This pressure is released when the molten rock flows up from the depths of the earth.

UNDER PRESSURE

Gases, liquids, and solids are affected in different ways when pressure is applied to them. Gases will attempt to escape from the pressure, but if they can't, they then begin to compress—their molecules squash closer together to take up less room. If the pressure is increased, the molecules cram so closely together that the gas eventually becomes a liquid.

This principle gives us a useful way of transporting gases. For example, the gas we use to heat our homes and to cook our food can be pressurized and transported in its liquid form to remote areas. Canisters of liquid gas are also used for camping stoves, portable heaters, or even hot-air balloons.

If liquids are subjected to a force of pressure, they will also attempt to escape. However, if liquids are trapped, they cannot compress like gases. Their molecules are already close together, so instead of compressing, they are said to "pressurize" as the force becomes distributed evenly throughout the trapped fluid. An aerosol spray is a canister of pressurized liquid mixed with a compressed gas that helps to force the liquid out as a spray mist.

Solids can also become pressurized, but unlike liquids, they do not need to become trapped to do so. Mounting pressure can cause solids to heat up, and the greater the pressure, the greater the heat generated. Solids will eventually melt if enough pressure is exerted. This is why some rocks turn to magma (molten rock) under Earth's crust. The great pressure of Earth's crust on the rocks below turns some of them into a liquid.

ATMOSPHERIC PRESSURE

Every cubic yard (1 cu m) of air contains about 27 million, million, million, million molecules. The air in the atmosphere contains a number of gases that are mixed together as the molecules move around. Just as the force of gravity pulls us toward the ground, gravity attracts the air molecules to Earth's surface. Air pressure is strongest near the ground because the air molecules have to bear the weight of all the molecules above them. This weight causes the air to compress, and it exerts pressure onto Earth's surface and other nearby objects. As you walk around each day, there is a huge weight above your head. Luckily, the pressure of our bodies counteracts this weight, so we don't feel it.

▲ Air pressure is very important in weather forecasting. When pressure is high, the air is heavy and sinks toward Earth. This usually means sunny weather because clouds find it difficult to rise when the air is pushing down. When the pressure is low, the air is a little lighter, and clouds form easily. When the pressure is really low, stormy weather is possible.

As you move away from Earth's surface, the air pressure decreases. Air pressure can differ at the same altitude because air molecules are also affected by changes in temperature. Warm air expands because the air molecules move around more than cold air molecules. Expanded air actually has a lower **density** than cold air, but it has a higher atmospheric pressure because it tries to push neighboring air molecules out of the way to make room. Barometers measure changes in the force of air pressure. They are used to detect weather patterns caused by changing air pressure.

▲ Barometers are used to measure changes in the force of air pressure. A vacuum in the barometer expands or contracts as the air pressure changes. This movement is transferred to a pointer and scale through a series of levers.

Low atmospheric pressure farther from Earth's surface.

High atmospheric pressure near Earth's surface.

PRESSURE EQUALIZATION

If you move to a different altitude, your body experiences changes in air pressure. If this happens slowly (such as when you climb up or down a hill), your body has time to adjust, and you won't really notice. However, when it happens quickly, such as when you fly off the ground in an airplane, you may sense a change of pressure in your ears. This is because your inner ear contains air that changes in pressure. When climbing (or ascending) in altitude, the eardrum begins to bend outward because the pressure inside the ear is greater than on the outside. The opposite happens when climbing down (or descending) in altitude. This can be uncomfortable until the ears "pop" so that the pressure is equalized by the passage of air through the eustachian tubes, which join the inner ears to the throat.

Changes in altitude can also make you feel unwell. As altitude increases, the air pressure lowers, and there are fewer oxygen molecules in the air to breathe. If the body hasn't been able to adjust to these changes, "altitude sickness" can occur. Symptoms include headaches, fatigue, shortness of breath, nausea, and a loss of appetite. Mountain climbers, hikers, and skiers are most at risk. If climbers get altitude sickness, they climb down to a lower altitude for a few days, where there is more oxygen in the air. This gives their body time to adjust before they begin to climb up again more slowly. The symptoms usually go away within a few days.

▼ Climbing at high altitude can bring problems of changing air pressure and density. Mountain climbers ascend slowly so that their bodies have time to adjust.

IN TOO DEEP

The effects of pressure underwater can be even more dramatic. If divers hold their breath, the water pressure compresses the air in their lungs, and their chests shrink in size as they go deeper underwater. The lungs of free divers can reduce to the size of oranges during a very deep dive.

When divers use oxygen tanks, the air pressure in their lungs matches the pressure of the water outside so that they can inhale and exhale properly. If deep-sea divers rise to the surface too quickly, however, the sudden drop in water pressure can cause nitrogen gas from the air cylinders to dissolve and form bubbles in their blood. This is extremely painful and is commonly known as "the bends" because it makes the body double up in agony. Deep-sea divers come to the surface slowly to prevent this from happening, but if they get the bends, they can spend time in a decompression chamber. This slowly equalizes the pressure so that the nitrogen gas leaves safely through the lungs.

▼ Divers can breathe underwater using pressurized tanks of oxygen.

UNDER STRAIN

When objects experience extreme pressure changes but cannot equalize them, more dramatic things can happen. If the force of pressure is greater inside, an outward explosion occurs. For example, fireworks are caused by a buildup of pressure as superheated gases and flames explode from the center. If the force of pressure is greater on the outside, a violent burst occurs inward. This is called an implosion. For example, if a submarine was deep underwater and began to lose air pressure due to a leak, it would become crushed by the pressure of the water on the outside. Brittle materials, such as glass, allow pressure to build up until they suddenly give way. When flexible materials are subjected to intense pressure, they either stretch or collapse completely.

DID YOU KNOW?

▶ The pressure of the atmosphere and the ocean water on the sea floor causes Earth to wobble and shift by about 23 feet (7 m) approximately every 400 days. Astronomers communicating with satellites orbiting Earth need to be aware of this shift and take it into consideration when they try to trace radio signals from their satellites.

▶ Car windshields can break if they are subjected to sudden pressure, such as the force of a stone from the road.

POPTASTIC

Scientists have found that making popcorn in conditions of low air pressure creates larger, fluffier popcorn and reduces the number of unpopped kernels. Popcorn is a type of corn made of starch (a form of carbohydrate) surrounded by a hard shell. When the kernel is heated, the water inside the kernel mixes with the starch and creates a jelly-like substance. Eventually, the water reaches its boiling point and begins to turn into a gas (steam). As the molecules of steam expand, the pressure increases, and eventually the kernel's shell splits under the force. As the steam expands inside the kernel, it pushes the jelly-like starch substance outward. On contact with the air, however, the pressure slowly decreases, and the popcorn stops expanding. Scientists now know that reducing the pressure of the outside air enables the popcorn to expand farther before this balance of forces is achieved.

8

Machines

When you look at the world around you, it is amazing to think how humans have been able to achieve so much when they themselves can lift only relatively small weights! From buildings made from big stone slabs to houses built at the top of steep mountains, humans have found some way of moving heavy materials. And this isn't just because of the technology and machinery we have today. Ancient man also managed to lift great weights—consider the statues on Easter Island. How did our ancestors manage to move such heavy loads?

▲ A nail sticking out of a piece of wood is difficult to take out with your fingers, but using a hammer can multiply the strength of the force you apply.

LEVERS

Levers are simple machines. They are used in all sorts of situations to provide a means of turning, lifting, lowering, or shifting things that would otherwise be difficult or impossible to hold and move. Levers are able to make a job easier because they have the effect of multiplying the force that is exerted on an object.

Consider a closed can of paint. The lid is very difficult to ease off with your fingernails. However, if you put a screwdriver under the lip of the lid and push downward on the edge of the can, you will find that the lid soon comes away very easily. Think of the screwdriver as a seesaw—the downward force of the effort causes the load on the other side to move up. Similarly, you can use a hammer as a lever to lift a nail from a piece of wood. You move the handle a large distance, but the hammerhead converts this into a larger force over a small distance.

Ancient man used levers in a similar way to lift heavy rocks. Just like the paint example above, placing a stick underneath a rock and pushing down on one end causes the rock to lift more easily. The longer the lever, the easier the job will be.

▲ These massive stone statues, on average more than 20 feet (6 m) high, can be found on Easter Island, a remote island in the Pacific Ocean. It is thought that the stones were transported and sculpted in the 1400s. How the stones were actually lifted remains a mystery.

Other examples of simple machines that use the action of levers include wheelbarrows, scissors, door hinges, and wrenches. Even your arm is a lever that moves from your elbow.

Levers always have a fixed point of rotation (the **fulcrum** or pivot) so that the force we apply is translated into a circular motion called "**torque**." Torque is measured in foot-pounds (or Newton-meters). Equal movements on either side of a fulcrum mean that the forces are balanced (like a seesaw that is level). Unbalanced forces cause the lever to move in a clockwise or counterclockwise direction.

INVESTIGATE

▶ There are examples of levers in everyday life. Look around your home and see how many you can identify.

Remember that some levers may be hidden (for example, a door handle is a lever). Don't forget, too, that the human body includes a number of levers and fulcrums—how many can you count?

EVERYDAY OBJECTS THAT USE LEVERS

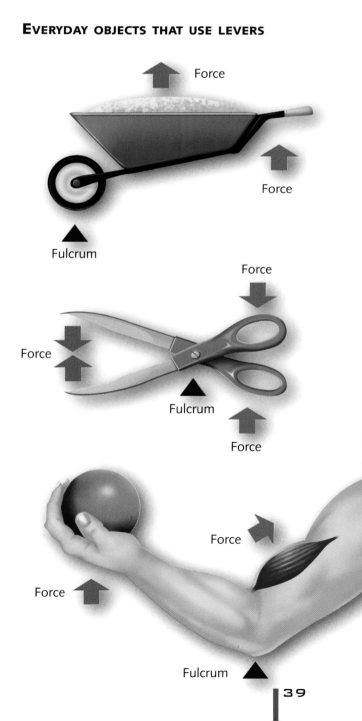

Machines are being created all the time to make our lives easier. Machines reduce the effort required to perform tasks or spread the effort so that a task is more manageable.

Around four million years ago, our ancestors had evolved into ape-like creatures that walked on two legs and had their hands free to perform new tasks. Our first true ancestors, called *Homo habilis*, developed a culture of making simple stone tools and weapons, which were used to convert the strength of their muscles into other, more useful forces. *Homo habilis* found that stone implements would help kill, skin, and butcher animals, or chop and shape pieces of wood. Since those times, technology has evolved, just as *Homo habilis* eventually evolved into *Homo sapiens*—our own species.

Over time, people developed a natural understanding of the way forces worked, even though they didn't understand forces in a scientific way. Early technology saw the invention of the lever and the wheel long before anyone had a grasp of the physics involved. People learned about existing technologies through teaching and by watching their elders, along with the trial and error of trying things for themselves.

Before long, man began to make more advanced machinery, based on the discoveries of his ancestors. Many of these machines utlilized the strength of natural forces: windmills used the force of the wind to pump water, grind corn, or generate electricity; water mills used the force of rivers for similar purposes; and sailboats used the force of the wind to move and transport people or goods. But man has gone one step further, and many machines now rely on mechanical forces generated by electricity. These machines have helped us to build and produce on a massive scale, advancing our civilization significantly.

▲ This digger uses a series of levers and a mechanical force from an engine to move and lift heavy pieces of rock on a building site.

▼ **Nodding donkeys are used to pump oil from deep beneath Earth's surface.**

Some of the machines that are used today help us get materials to make new machines or to produce energy to power machinery. For example, a nodding donkey is a type of pump used to take oil from the ground. A pump is a mechanical device used to move liquids or gases. Pumps use mechanical forces to push the material up by pressure or by suction.

A nodding donkey is usually driven by a motor and "nods" at regular intervals. It has a metal rod connecting the head to a pump, located thousands of feet underground. On the downward stroke, the piston moves down and compresses the air in the pump, forcing fluid to come out. On the upstroke, the piston is pushed back out again, expanding the area so that fluid is sucked into the pipe. These pumps are often used to extract onshore oil reserves (as opposed to oil found under the seabed). They can extract up to 10.5 gallons (40 L) of an oil and water mixture with each stroke.

Another area of our lives in which machinery has produced a significant transformation is the textile industry. Our constant need for clothing has meant that for centuries wool fiber has been spun into yarn, and threads have been woven into cloth. However, in the 1700s, the textile industry developed dramatically. Before this time, almost every item of clothing was handmade. Goods that were made to be strong and durable took a long time to make and were very expensive. Then, in the 1730s, a new device called the "flying shuttle" meant that loom workers no longer had to weave thread by hand. The shuttle was powered by a lever, and its mechanical force increased the productivity of weaving enormously.

As cloth became easier to make, it also became less expensive to buy. Later, in the 1700s, the invention of the "spinning jenny" meant that it also became possible to produce finer and stronger yarns on a large scale. This machine enabled a worker to spin eight threads at once by turning a single wheel.

Then, in 1851, the invention of the first practical sewing machine (by American Isaac Singer) revolutionized the lives of many people, who began to make clothes and other products for themselves. The first sewing machines were designed with a wheel that turned levers. Today, they are powered by electricity.

▼ **The invention of the sewing machine in the 1850s made it possible to make clothes at home.**

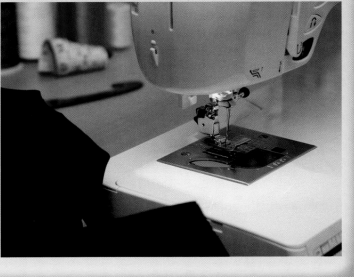

9

Stresses and strains

When engineers, architects, and designers begin their work, they need to take into account forces when deciding on suitable structures, shapes, and materials for their products. Materials deal with forces in different ways.

▶ This bulletproof glass can withstand extreme forces. It has been made by layering pieces of plastic between the glass to make it stronger.

A material is said to be "tough" if it survives the shock of being hit by another object. An object that is "brittle" (the opposite of tough) shatters, tears, or breaks apart upon impact or after resulting shock waves. The strength of materials is tested thoroughly before they are made into different products, and items also have to pass strict safety standards before they are sold. Glass is often known to shatter on impact. However, scientists have now found ways to toughen glass—for example, in car windshields or in security doors—so that this transparent material maintains its shape under extreme pressure. Glass-reinforced plastic (GRP) is a combination of glass and plastic mixed together. Individually, the two materials are not particularly strong, but when used together, they make a very tough, lightweight, and flexible material.

▶ This machine is testing the strength of the saucepan's handle. The machine lifts the saucepan up and down repeatedly by the handle and checks for any damage.

▲ The cables of the Golden Gate bridge in San Francisco are 3 feet (0.9 m) in diameter and more than 6,560 feet (2,000 m) in length. They are held by two towers and support vertical cables that carrry the weight of the road below.

▲ When walls are built, different brick patterns can be used to maximize the strength of the building.

Strength and weakness are terms used to describe the property of materials that can withstand a force over a long period of time. The bricks in buildings are said to have "compression strength" because they can withstand being squashed between two forces that push against each other. Alternatively, the cable holding a suspension bridge is said to possess "tensile strength" because it can withstand being pulled by two forces moving away from each other. "Shear strength" is the ability of a material to withstand a twisting, rotating, or shearing force, while a material with "elastic strength" changes shape under stress but will always return to its original shape once the forces are removed.

▶ Diamonds are very valuable and are often desired as an item of jewelry. Relatively few diamonds are found on Earth's surface, where they formed billions of years ago deep underground. Diamonds are also the hardest natural substance known to man.

Hardness is used to describe an object's resistance to being scratched. If an object is hard-wearing, then it will not scratch or mark very easily, unless it is in contact with something harder. Softness is a relative term because an object is soft only in comparison to a harder object. Diamonds are the hardest natural substance on Earth. The word "diamond" comes from a Greek word meaning "invincible." Diamonds are most commonly known for their desirability in the jewelry trade. However, around 80 percent of the diamonds that are mined annually are used in industry. Their hardness means that they can be used to cut, grind, and polish other hard substances without wearing out.

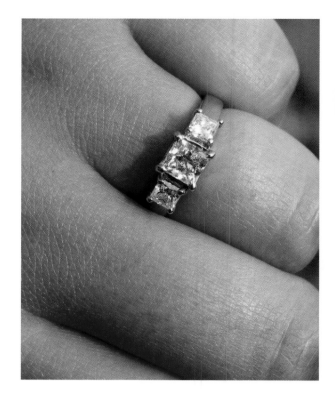

▼ Diamonds are so hard that they can only be cut using another diamond. This diamond is being shaped using a diamond grinding wheel with a thin layer of diamond grain on its surface that acts as an abrasive.

Time travel: Into the future

One of the strongest materials known to man is spider silk. A spider's drag-line silk can support more than 14,500 pounds (6,500 kg) per square inch (6.5 sq cm)—much more than a steel wire of the same thickness. Besides being strong, spider silk is also quite elastic, stretching up to 40 percent of its normal length. The silk can also retain its strength at temperatures as low as -76 °F (-60 °C). Most other materials become brittle and tend to "snap" at such extreme temperatures. Spider silk would be ideal for making products in which strength and lightness are important. For example, the silk could be used to make stronger and lighter bulletproof vests and lightweight parachute cords that maintain their strength at the freezing temperatures of high altitudes. However, spider silk takes such a long time to harvest that it is too expensive to make at the moment. However, scientists in the U.S. have figured out how to **genetically modify** the mammary glands of goats with the **DNA** from orb weaving spiders. Their work suggests that in the future, it may be possible to manufacture spider silk in quantities that were never thought possible before. Engineers are always on the lookout for miniature materials that are tough enough to advance technologies using computer chips and **microsurgery**. In the 1990s, the creation of nanotubes made this dream a reality. Nanotubes are tiny tubes about 10,000 times thinner than a human hair. They are made of cylinders of carbon molecules. Nanotubes are thought to be the strongest material (for their weight) known to man—10 times stronger than steel and about a quarter of the weight. In the future, nanotubes could be used in the development of materials for buildings, cars, airplanes, and even thread for ultra-strong fabric or clothing. They are also as flexible as plastic and a good conductor of electricity—the perfect material for minute wires that can be used in ultrasmall electronic devices.

▼ The creation of nanotubes in the 1990s is set to revolutionize the electronics industry. Minute wires made from nanotubes can make electronic devices smaller than ever.

▲ Spider silk is remarkably strong. It is also light and elastic, making it an ideal material from which to make things. For this reason, scientists are working hard to find a way to harvest it in large quantities.

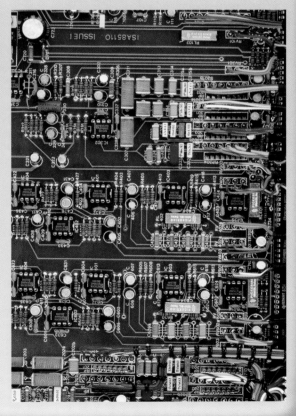

Glossary

ACCELERATION – The rate at which speed is changed.

AERODYNAMIC – Designed to reduce wind resistance. Also known as "streamlined."

AIRFOIL – A surface, such as an aircraft wing, that is shaped to produce lift when air flows over and under it.

ATMOSPHERE – The mass of air that surrounds Earth.

BUOYANCY – The upward force on an object immersed in a liquid or a gas, enabling it to float or appear to become lighter.

COMPRESS – To squeeze together so that a gas or solid takes up less space.

DECOMPRESSED – Relieved of compression.

DENSITY – The mass of a substance compared to its volume.

DNA (DEOXYRIBONUCLEIC ACID) – A substance in the nucleus of each living cell that holds all of the inherited characteristics of the plant or animal.

FRICTION – A force that slows down movement and produces heat.

FULCRUM – The supporting point from which a lever turns. Also called the pivot.

GENETICALLY MODIFY – To change the genetic structure of a living organism.

GLIDERS – Aircraft without engines that fly using rising currents of hot air.

GRAVITY – The force that pulls all materials together across space.

GYRATE – To move in a spiral around a fixed point.

HANG GLIDER – A type of aircraft consisting of a large nylon wing, equipped with a harness from which a rider hangs when gliding from a height.

HYDRODYNAMIC – Designed to reduce water resistance. Also known as "streamlined."

HYDROFOIL – A surface that is shaped to produce lift when water flows over and under it.

ANSWERS

page 12 Test yourself
The journey will take 2.5 hours.

page 24 Test yourself
Example answers:
Useful friction—friction between shoes and the ground, preventing you from slipping when walking; friction between your fingers and a pencil, helping you to grip a pencil to write or draw; friction between a pencil and paper, helping you to write or draw; friction between your bottom and the chair, preventing you from slipping off your seat; friction between a chair and the floor, helping the chair to stay in one place; friction between a wet finger and the pages of a book, helping you to turn the page; friction between car tires and the road, preventing the car from skidding; friction between a match and the side of a matchbox to produce a flame; friction between sandpaper and wood, helping to produce a smooth surface.

Nuisance friction—friction between moving machinery, causing defects or damage; friction between a comb and wet hair (hair conditioner can act as a lubricant, helping the comb to move more easily); friction in a car engine, producing heat and requiring extra fuel to power the vehicle; friction making it difficult to slide a box across the floor; friction making it difficult to ride a bicycle (or walk) through deep snow; friction of moving air in a car with the window open, requiring extra fuel to power the vehicle; a machine overheating due to friction; the soles of your shoes wearing out due to friction.

page 39 Test yourself
Example answers—scissors, door handle, scale, toilet handle, bottle opener, nutcracker, tongs, pliers, nail clippers, crowbar, spade, bicycle brakes, wheelbarrow, fishing rod, oars of a boat, your forearm, your knee, your ankle, your back.

INERTIA – The tendency for an object to stay in the same state, whether it is at rest or continuing to move in a straight line. A force is needed to overcome inertia.

LEVERS – Simple machines used for lifting weights or prying something open.

LIFT – To raise or pick up an object.

LUBRICANTS – Slippery substances, such as oil or grease, used to coat the surfaces of the moving parts of a machine. Lubricants allow them to move forward smoothly against each other and reduce friction.

MASS – The amount of matter in an object.

MATTER – The material of which all things are made.

MICROSURGERY – Surgery on tiny parts of the body, performed with the aid of a microscope and other specialized instruments.

MOLECULES – Two or more atoms joined together.

MOTION – Movement from place to place.

ORBITING – Traveling around another object.

PARACHUTES – Large, umbrella-shaped devices made of fabric. Parachutes are used to slow down the speed at which a person or object falls through the air.

PRESSURE – The force that a solid, gas, or liquid exerts on another object or surface that it touches. Pressure is measured in pounds per square inch (or pascals).

RESISTANCE – Something that acts against a force, preventing or slowing down motion.

ROCKET – A cylinder-shaped device that is propelled by hot gases. Fuel is burned in a chamber inside the rocket to produce gases that escape through the rear vent and drive the rocket forward or upward.

SATELLITE – An object in orbit around a larger object in space. The moon is a satellite of Earth. Artificial satellites circling around Earth are used to reflect radio signals and to forecast the weather.

SPACE PROBES – Spacecraft carrying instruments used to explore objects in space.

SPACE SHUTTLE – A spacecraft that takes off like a rocket, flies like a spacecraft, and lands like a glider. It can be used again and again.

SPACECRAFT – Any spaceship or satellite designed to travel in space.

SPEED – The rate at which something moves.

TELESCOPES – Optical instruments with lenses or mirrors that magnify distant objects.

TIDE – The regular rise and fall of the surface of the oceans caused by the pull of the sun and moon.

TORQUE – The force provided by a lever.

WEIGHT – The force with which something is attracted to Earth.

Index

Page references in italics represent pictures.

DATE DUE

Demco, Inc. 38-293